Heartfelt Words

Words Speak When Hearts Cannot

A book of poetry by
Teresa Short Mitchell

Meroe Publishing

Heartfelt Words

Meroe Publishing

3

DEDICATION

I *dedicate this book to my deceased father, Timothy Short, Sr. who was killed when I was 9 years old and my mother, Ardella Short who has taught by example, the power of faith.*

Protecting my honor, defending my heart,
Pain deep within is what I am trying to avoid.
          - -Teresa Mitchell

ABOUT THE AUTHOR/Acknowledgements

Teresa Short Mitchell was born the third of ten children and reared in Brooklyn, Georgia (the outskirt of the small town of Richland), graduated from Stewart County High School, Tuskegee Institute (now University), and Troy State University, holds an Educational Specialist degree, has served as an administrator with Harris County and Fulton County Schools, and resides in the Atlanta Metropolitan area.

Contents

Love and Relationships

Motivation and Inspiration

Heartfelt Words

This book is broken into two sections. In the first section, love is explored through a multitude of fluctuating emotions to include joy, happiness, success, peace as well as hurt, pain, conflict, anguish and disappointment.

In the second section, words are used to reach into the depths of the inner spirit to provide inspirational support, emotional stability and motivation for individuals to hold steadfast to their convictions.

SPEAK TO MY HEART

Speak to my heart, whisper softly, or it could shatter
and break,
Speak to my heart with genuine love, not words that
are fake;

Speak to my heart, tell it how our ship has sailed to
discover,
That the love we have belongs only to each other;

Speak to my heart, in a low mellow tone,
And if the biddings right, my heart you will forever
own;

Speak to my heart, so I will know you are near,
Say you care for me more and more, so it is
apparently clear;

That I am the gem in your crown,
And I will be precious to you and our relationship
sound.

SPEAK...SPEAK TO MY HEART...NOW.

Moments With You Are Priceless

Being around you provides lightness to my heart,
So much that I miss you terribly when we are apart;

The sparkle in your eyes provides a guiding light,
That acts as a beacon when I look into them each
night;

You spread warmth when you smile and walk in any
room,
Heads turn, and everyone focuses on my lover, they
presume.

This moment with you is priceless.

As you move throughout the room, your grace people
mention,
Your beauty is the focal point, but your voice
commands attention;

I am proud to escort such a wonderful person on my
arms,
I stand in awe at how mesmerized others are with
your charm.

This moment with you is priceless.

It used to bother me not to be where your attention
was directed,
But now that our moments alone are priceless, I have
adjusted;

I will never be able to figure out what someone like
you sees in me,
So I thank GOD everyday for allowing it to be;

Because...
My moments with you are priceless.

DARLING

From the moment you touched me, I knew there was no turning back,
I felt your strength, interpreted your vibes, I can't deny these facts;

You have touched me deep within, taken me from a world of torment,
And though I know it won't last forever, I am enjoying every moment;

Things are going so well, but moving too fast,
I am caught in this whirlwind, wondering how long things will last;

Feelings, urges, and desires that I had brushed from my mind,
You, you have unleashed them in such a short period of time;

Are you a demon from hell…an imitation of love or
An angel from heaven, a reality, pure love?

Whatever you are, you have saved my body, soul, and heart from starving,
So much do you mean to me, your name shall be simply…DARLING.

Cut Like Glass

I love him so much that I try hard to be strong,
But sometimes because of what he says, I would
rather be alone;

How do I move on? How do I get past…
The things he's done, the words he says, when they
continue to cut like glass?

How do I grin and bear it? I forgive, but I can't
forget,
The things he's done, the words he says when they
continue to cut like glass;

Sometimes I feel I would be better off without him in
my life,
But he has this hold over me, I can't imagine not
being his wife;

Oh God, help me leave everything that has happened
to me behind,
Show me how to gain the peace that I want in my
heart and mind;

Please help me to get past the things he's done, the
words he says, so they no longer cut like glass.

PERHAPS...My Search Is Over

Special occasions have always been important in my
life,
But for so long I have been hurt, hell I'll even say
deprived;

All I ever wanted was to find someone to put my
feelings first,
Someone to care for me, love me, and quench my
mind's thirst;

Someone full of life, fun, and substance,
Someone to appreciate who I am and accept my
words for instance;

For my words speak of hurt, anger, frustration and
pain,
They come from a heart tarnished with such a deep
stain;

That only true love can come in and remove,
This heartache that I have with passion as the tool;

You are that tool that's gently twisted, turned, and
rearranged my life,
And I will be forever grateful because you helped me
to survive;

From the moment I first heard your voice, it's been
music to my ears,
Only the beauty of a newly budding rose could
compare to the way you make me feel.

PERHAPS...MY SEARCH IS OVER.

Handling Business

I know we are not at the place we thought we would
be,
I certainly never thought I would need you to make
my life complete;

By pulling your love from me, you have disrupted my
soul,
I am in a state of confusion and helplessness, with no
sense of control;

'Cause you can't handle your business.

I just want to understand why you treat me like
poison,
Explain it to me like I am a two year old, so I'll
understand your reason;

Can't you handle your business?

Lord knows I have tried to figure out if the problem is
your pride,
After much deliberation, I feel I have no choice but to
decide,
That what I thought we were building, only I felt
inside,
And you just came along for a temporary joy ride;

I guess that's how you handle your business!

How stupid I have been focusing on your body and
not your voice,
Accepting the way you treated me recently like I had
not choice;

I guess it is time for me to handle my business.

Let me see if I can sum this up so you and I both will
understand,
I don't need, desire, or intend to have a man in my
life who can't focus on being just my man;

I am making this clear so you know exactly where I
am coming from,
But just in case, simply speaking, "Get to stepping!"
keep moving, and get the hell on!

I am sure you understand,

It's Just Business!

SICK-N-TIRED

Tradition teaches us to find love and happiness will
follow,
But experience has taught me that love sometimes
isn't enough;

When you are sick-n-tired of hurting, asking for what
you want and feeling rejected,
It is easy to build walls and straddle fences as shields
when your needs are neglected;

And somehow you continue to love that person even
though it's a struggle to coexist,
Wanting desperately to be loved, and iron the
wrinkles out of the relationship;

But when you become sick-n-tired of ill treatment,
broken promises and prolific lies,
The constant bickering, the complain syndrome, and
the too often watery eyes;

You refuse to ignore the obvious signs that your
needs and wants are last on the list,
You start to demand better, because you realize your
relationship is amiss;

When you have continuously made adjustments,
compromised and now it is a sacrifice,
You walk away knowing it is okay to love but not live
with this person the rest of your life;

This is why I have given up on falling in love in hopes
of finding happiness,

17

I resolve from this day forward, I shall search for
happiness and learn to fall in love;

Because I find myself facing the reality that I am
sick-n-tired of being sick-n-tired,
When all I really want is to think of that special
person, sigh and smile.

Renewal of a Man's Vows

When time wears you down and your body gets weak,
And peace of mind is all that you seek;

When there is no place to hide or to rest,
And your burdens are heavy, will you pass the test?

Will you remember to love her, cherish her more,
The woman you say you love and adore?

Will you appreciate her kindness, cherish her love,
And remember to thank the good Lord above…

For sending her to you to share your life,
For allowing this woman to become your wife?

Will you continue to love her…and keep her close,
And commit to loving her even more?

If you do, you are on the right road,
And the road gets easier as time unfolds;

Because today is a celebration of the day it began,
Tell her you would marry her all over again.

No Right to Be Parked on Love's Driveway

I have no right to make requests from you,
The generosity you provide should be because you
want to;

I have no right to feel hurt or disappointment,
When I sense you have an interest in other women;

You have no ties to me and no stake in my heart,
I had nothing to gain in this from the start;

How do I turn my feelings off and move on with my
life and goals?
Who will I turn to now that this relationship has run
its course?

Knowing this doesn't make my heart hurt any less,
Nor does it release the overwhelming amount of
stress;

I am guilty of diving in feet first, but my eyes were
wide open,
Please don't patronize me, you can't blame a girl for
hoping;

That somehow, some way, things would work
themselves out,
I am left trying to figure out why a relationship
headed up, somehow went south;

Do I encompass my time and energy trying to pick
up the pieces,

Or do I close the door, and hope that this unbearable
pain eases;

I have no right to be parked on love's driveway,
Unless there is a deserving gentleman mending
hearts today;

With all of this occupying my mind, I open up a
search,
To determine if we should be driving, parking or
moving in reverse.

Deep Thoughts

I close my eyes and immediately you are there,
What I see, I need desperately for you to share;

My hands gently carve out your body in my mind,
You fall softly and helplessly in my arms and become
mine;

We relax and lay comfortably holding and caressing
each other,
So tranquilizing is the air, as we fulfill each other;

For I see us in a place untainted by misconceptions,
A place and time with no need for directions;

Perhaps when you miss me and the hole in your heart
grows large,
You will decide to share reality with me instead of
apart;

Maybe there is still time to rekindle the magic we
once shared,
Or maybe it's already too late, but I can't allow my
thoughts to go there;

You need to remember that I will wait, but only for so
long,
And no matter how you justify it, hurting me is
wrong;

I'm not an old set of keys you can throw away and
forget,
I think of how vocal and straight forward I have been
from the moment we met;

It is your turn to let your imagination run wild,
To allow your emotions to lose control for just a little
while;

If you remember your not so subtle approach and
strong desire,
To get close to me, to feel passion, to fuel the fire;

That has been burning until recently between us,
Imagine the touch, the kiss, being together is a must;

Will you let it fade or fight for what you want?
If you are not sure, your three downs are up, so punt;

Because these games you are playing cannot go on
this way,
And I won't allow my thoughts of you to tie me down
another day.

Divorce Prelude

As the tears well in the corners of my eyes,
What I am contemplating should come as no
surprise;

I know deep in my heart and sincerely in my mind,
That no matter how this ends, we will both survive;

We once loved each other and cared beyond what
words could express,
Yet we managed to allow our relationship to
disintegrate into this mess;

There was a time when you were my world, my
reason for living,
The vicious cycle of hurt, pain, and agony has made
me stop giving;

Especially since there is nothing left to give,
Except my freedom...if you will;

Allow me and yourself to see things like never before,
Try to genuinely accept the things your heart already
knows;

We instilled hope and devotion into the saying that
opposites attract,
But the love we shared has died and we will never get
it back;

No one is ever sure of what to do when the attraction
goes away,

Maybe some accept companionship and decide to stay;

But for me, I am going to take the road most traveled,
It will cement the fact that our lives, family and relationship are totally dismantled.

You're Not Strong Enough to Love Me

I gave my all to prove that you were special in my life,
I held so tightly to the moments that we shared, yet
they diminished over time;

I'm unique, have my own sense of style, unlike any
other fish in the ocean or sea,
I have my own agenda, and you're not strong enough
to love me;

I deserve more care and consideration than you will
ever provide,
So while you are fishing for yourself, I am going on
with my life;

You see, you don't deserve someone to give their all
to you completely,
And I deserve better, 'cause you're not strong enough
to love me;

You're not strong enough to love me and something
inside you is wrong,
And I don't have the time, patience or will to try and
overcome;

Whatever it is that is controlling you as you search for
the piece to make you whole,
You're not strong enough to love me, so in my life
you have no role;

No part in my life for you to keep putting down my
thoughts, ideas or decisions,
No more room for your words to cut like incisions;

I'm dynamite, I'm poison, I'm a potential fire,
You're not strong enough to love me, yet I am the
object of your desire;

I'm the one you yearn for and think of night and day,
But it can't be because I am not Burger King and you
can't have everything your way;

I am the one who sacrificed and put your butt
through school,
Now that you have that little education, you think you
have the right to change the rules;

Oh no, I need someone to stand beside me and do
right even if I say something wrong,
I need someone who after work has the decency to
come home;

Now I know, what for years others could see,
You're a poor excuse for a lover and you're not strong
enough to love me;

You don't have what it takes for me to love and
respect you through eternity,
The bottom line is…you're not strong enough to love
or appreciate me, for me.

Is It Me?

Is it me who has sent this relationship spiraling?
Is it me who has this relationship unraveling?

Is it me who has been so stupid or acted without sense?
Is this me doing my best thinking when the situation is tense?

Is it me who performs well under pressure and meets deadlines?
Is it me who never allows myself to be tested in my own life?

Is it me who wonders how to perform, react or even prepare,
For a man who for a short time pretended to care?

Is it me who should test the waters and allow myself to feel his touch?
Is it me who should reach for him, and let him have what he wants so much?

There is no argument from my conscience as my body suffers from love starvation,
I was fooling myself thinking I had remedied the situation;

Is it me who needs him to come clean if he cares for me like he pretends to?
It is me who needs him to seal the relationship by telling me the truth?

What do you think... *Is It Me?*

Two Fools

Look there, two fools taking turns looking back,
Two fools both scared to the point that they lack;

The confidence to step out on faith and what they
believe,
So they take turns deciding to pack up and leave;

Not because there is no respect for their love,
But because two fools are second guessing the
answer from above;

What a shame, they are missing out on so much,
Two fools brought together over and over by His
touch;

He has placed His blessing on their union, yet they
are afraid,
Whether it be career, education, finance or age;

They are prime examples of two fools,
Who keep looking for any answer to change the rules;

So they will be assured that their relationship will last
a lifetime,
Again, what a shame, these two fools are wasting the
gift of love and time;

Two fools. Are you one of the two?

You Have Touched Me

You have touched me with your eyes,
And I know that you sense what I feel inside;

You have touched me with your voice,
And made it clear that I made the right choice;

You have touched me with your hands,
And for me, you are the perfect man;

You have touched me deep inside with your charm,
And continue to caress me with the comfort of your
arms;

You have touched me with your presence,
Letting me know that you will be here today,
tomorrow and forever;

You have touched me and I know our love is real,
And we have grown to a point where our world is
surreal;

You have touched me and are embedded beneath my
skin,
And I want you to touch me over and over again;

Now you know how you have touched me.

I Don't Even Know Who I Am

I allowed my mind to wonder back one day,
Reminisce on my life as some might say;

I couldn't believe all the things I saw,
There wasn't one happy moment without a flaw;

All these years have come and gone,
And as miserable as I was, I still hung on;

Giving my all and trying to make things work,
And it still fell apart and gee, it hurts;

I don't even know who I am after all these years,
After running from the truth and dodging my fears;

I tried to be everything to someone else through the
role of wife,
So much that I sacrificed myself, compromised my
happiness and lost control of my own life;

I don't even know who I am for most of my adult life
I have been attached to a man,
I thought I was a strong, intelligent woman, yet I am
struggling to find answers and to understand;

How somehow I got lost in the shuffle, the
commitment of love,
And with no confidence I was waiting for an answer
from above;

Obviously I never got the answer I was hoping or
looking for,
That's one reason I still don't know who I am and
keep anticipating just one more;

One more, different answer, the one I can accept,
The one I want the powers that be to give, to change
how I felt;

I slept through an adult life not making the decisions
I needed to make,
For fear I would destroy someone else's world or by
some chance break;

Someone else's heart, forsaking my own heart and
feelings,
Though deep inside, my heart, my soul and thoughts
were screaming;

I am not happy! I just want to be happy!
I don't even know who I am, or what it means to be
me;

As I try to break away and finally be strong,
I know I will be the bad guy, the one they say is
wrong;

For breaking up a marriage, for being selfish this
way,
I feel guilty but I want let myself be unhappy another
day;

This is my opportunity to define myself and discover
peace,
To uncover the true person that I am underneath;

Because right now... I don't even know who I am.

A Prayer Fulfilled

The smile on your face, the touch of your hand,
AND the words spoken from a confident man;

The request to spend more time together,
To accompany me to church, my how clever;

Time spent afterwards enjoying each other's
company,
Laughing, talking, and sharing experiences so
openly;

A get-to-know me session, a prayer being fulfilled,
Peace of mind forthcoming, two hearts totally
thrilled;

The promise of love that will span a lifetime,
The confirmation of a relationship where I'm yours
and you're mine;

The joy you've instilled in my life is unbelievable,
Because the love we share is nothing short of a
miracle;

I thank GOD for allowing me to visualize this fantasy,
For answering my prayer and making it a reality;

You are my knight in armor, I am your sunshine on a
cloudy day,
From friends to lovers to a place where our hearts will
never stray;

It is my prayer that we continue to share feelings and moments always,

Thus, A PRAYER FULFILLED.

A Prayer Fulfilled

was written especially for the love of my life.

COME TO ME

Come to me, bring your heart,
Leave it with me, this is where we start;

Come to me, bring your soul,
From this our love and lives we will mold;

Come to me, bring your mind,
Mix it with your heart and soul, so they intertwine;

Come to me, bring your body,
Together, our future shall be bright, not cloudy;

Come to me, bring your emotions,
For this, I promise you everlasting love and devotion;

Come to me with your heart, soul and your emotions
in hand,
And in return, I will provide your mind and body with
more love than your spirit can withstand.

COME TO ME.

To Judge a Book by It's Cover

A genuine lover is not what you'll discover,
If you try to judge a book by its cover;

Just because it's attractive and you are drawn to it,
Doesn't mean you will like what's written on the
pages;

To read a person well, you have to learn their
personality,
Use their words and deeds to evaluate their quality;

Just stop, think, and ask yourself,
"Would I like to be judged by someone else?"

By the love, anguish, or disappointment on your face,
Some of you realize it could lead to disgrace;

Give that person a chance, who knows how they have
grown,
You could ensure yourself of not living a lifetime
alone;

Never sell yourself short of a possible lover,
Just because you decided to judge a book by its
cover.

Forgive Me

Forgive me for not wanting to leave the comfort of
your arms,
Forgive me for allowing myself to succumb to your
charm;

Forgive me for trying to build a relationship simply
on love and trust,
Forgive me for thinking there was something special
between us;

Forgive me for desiring to feel your touch,
For wanting to hear your voice and love you so much;

Forgive me for just being me,
But it is the only way I know to be,
Perhaps you have already forgiven and forgotten
about me;

Forgive me for believing I could trust you as I do
myself,
For thinking I could make a difference in your life
like no one else;

Forgive me for infringing on your family and life,
And for the role I played taking time from your wife;

It was all done in hopes of finding happiness,
I forgive myself for thinking you were different from
the rest.

Twists of Fate

Tears came into my big, beautiful, yet sad eyes and
welled,
But I held strong, steadfast, pushed back the tears
and not a single drop fell;

As I thought of our first few encounters and how we
casually met,
How we created some great memories, ones we will
never forget;

Things didn't go bad, they just couldn't stay great,
We came from two different worlds, but I thought I
had finally found my soul mate;

It was fate that brought us together for the wonderful
moments we shared,
And I am better off believing that you actually cared;

Even for the little while you were here in my life,
I can hold my head high, look forward and take it all
in stride;

For I feel good about myself and what I stand for,
Even though I can't hold and love you anymore;

I know what I felt and the moments we shared were
not illusions,
Yet we are giving up on love and us while we sort
through the confusion;

Without warning fate steps in and takes its turn,
We don't control it, it controls us, this I've learned.

A Shaky Start

My eyes watered immediately after we said our vows,
If our marriage is so great, why are my eyes blurry
now;

One day short of a year and the pain continues to be
there,
He says he loves me, but he doesn't show he cares;

My heart aches for kind words and his gentle touch,
A sensitive response, a simple caress from him,
obviously too much;

I am faced with the choice of what to do right now,
With the man I said I do, I will, I vow;

Patience has been my constant shortcoming and
downfall,
Strong will and independence my strength, but those
are not all;

God has given me all I need to move forward with my
life,
Shucks, I now believe I am not cut out to be his wife;

I said that once, no, wait, twice,
Before the third time, I must realize;

Am I meant to live my life in solitude?
If I change my thinking, then I change my attitude;

I need to gather my thoughts, let go, you know... find
me,

But that would mean I would have to get a divorce
decree;

Better now than later, this way I choose my own road,
When I take the bull by the horns, I am the one in
control;

I am the one who allowed him into my life,
It was me who decided to vow to be his wife;

It is a shaky start and we are in need of guidance,
He says he is sorry, gives kisses, but all without
romance;

What a lousy situation to find myself in,
Because whatever I do, I will lose, not win.

Forbidden Fruit

I used to pray that my marriage would work out,
I had done this before and taken a different route;

Going outside my marriage is not something I am
thinking of lightly,
I have fought for my marriage, gave all I could, now I
want to be free;

After being approached by different men again and
again,
I now think I may be acquainted with just the right
man;

There's just one drawback, we are both forbidden
fruit,
And trying to pretend it doesn't matter is of no use;

My mind fills with lo-o-o-o-nging thoughts of him,
My body aches with passion, my thoughts should be
condemned;

I fantasize about us spending all day in bed,
But common sense keeps these thoughts in my head;

I know not to take a bit of forbidden fruit even when I
am weak,
The consequences are too great, the pleasure short-
lived, and I would constantly have to sneak;

To know this hurts, yet it feels good to know,
If I should take a piece, the fruit would be so--sweet.

Just Let Me Know

Take the time to jot a note or even send a letter,
A short message from you sure would make things
better;

Better for you in my heart and for me in my mind,
It would be better for both of us, if you just took the
time;

To show me you care as you say you do,
Prove to me beyond a doubt that your love is true;

Reassure me that you will always be there,
Make me believe that you really do care;

I just want to hear your voice or see your face,
It is as though you have disappeared without a trace;

Are you planning to be here for me or is your soul
lost?
Shall I reach to save our love again and at what cost?

The price goes higher and I get weaker each time I
struggle to reach,
I have learned several lessons, but what did I teach?

To lower my standards and expectations, to become
your rug,
To place everything on the table in exchange for true
love;

Whichever it is, be man enough to inform me of your decision,
If you are out of my life, then put our love out of commission;

Just let me know so I can move on with my life,
Do something formidable and let go of your pride.

Just Let Me Know.

Time to Say Good Bye

For weeks you have treated me like I do not exist,
My pride will not let you or any man, treat me like
this;

You have kept me at arms length, at bay, I say,
I have had a man before that treated me this way;

Thanks for the ride, I'm terminating your role,
And I will recover from this by healing my soul;

It is apparently clear, out of sight, out of mind,
So I want you to disappear, taking no more of my
time;

No matter what you say or how you deny,
I realize that it is time to say good bye;

If I should see you around, I will pretend you don't
exist,
Because I know you and that's just the way it is;

Continue to meet and converse with your friends,
But make sure you tell the truth about how our story
ends;

Tell them you followed their directions and said what
they wanted you to say,
Tell them I responded by quickly turning, walking,
then running away;

Tell them I would not stand idly by,
Instead I thought, then said, it's time to say good
bye.

Rationally Thinking

I cannot get you out of my mind, with every breath I
take, my thoughts are of you,
I wonder if you toss and turn, think of me and have
sleepless nights too;

You are my last thought before I go to bed,
When I rise, you're the first thought in my head;

There is something electrifying happening, some
powerful, gravitating force,
Controlling my emotions, so I feel I have no choice;

No matter what I say or whatever I may do,
This compelling force is inevitably driving me to you;

You said one of us must remain rational at all times,
As difficult as it is to admit, I want you to be
rightfully mine;

I trust you, lone for you, and crave you more and
more,
But I am losing control of my thoughts, and rationally
thinking isn't as important anymore;

We have thought about it and been strong enough to
stop ourselves,
And as pleasant as the act could be, we don't have the
right to hurt anyone else;

Especially the people we care for and say we love so,
They are the ones we must think of now and see each
other no more.

LOVE NOTE

As the time passes and our memories are no longer clear,
I continue to think of you and can't hold back the tears;

The days we spent together, the nights we shared,
Nothing slipped up on us, yet we weren't prepared;

To lose what we thought we had steadily built,
Time just hasn't washed away the compelling guilt;

It just doesn't seem right for us to be apart,
But we both know there is no easy way to mend a broken heart;

Maybe it is good that we are no longer together,
Since we were having such a hard time withstanding the weather;

Life storms were so strong our love was swept away,
And though months have past, I still desire you to this day;

I am concluding in my mind, I have to set this man free,
If he doesn't come back, then it wasn't meant to be.

Promises, Promises

When you first approached me, it was an awkward
situation,
We had both been celebrating a special occasion;

We danced, talked, and danced some more,
Until our heads, bodies and minds were spinning
above the floor;

You said all the right things and touched all the right
places,
Your cool, collective demeanor never ceases to amaze
me;

So soft your touch, so warm your kiss,
As we nestled together like fingers in a fist;

Could this man love me, I really want a response,
No matter what the answer, I would still write pros
and cons;

Before I could asked, he said, "You are all that
matters,"
I hung on every word as the room was filled with
chatter;

I wish I could put all my cards on the table,
So I would know if what we're facing is fact, fiction,
fairy tale or fable;

Right now you are promising to always be there for
me,
Yet the next words you speak are how much you
enjoy being free;

What will be my true place in your organized life,
Will I progress from friend, to lover, perhaps wife?

You console and reassure me of your love no matter
what,
I remind myself that we are not kids, but consenting
adults;

Sure we can promise to be together and find time to
get away,
Yet in my mind, I am hoping, dreaming that you will
be mine someday;

You promise it will happen, just wait, I will see,
We end the same way, a forehead kiss and a hug
that's barely friendly;

Once again the night is over, ending our little thrill,
Leaving only your photograph to prove you are real.

Yet...You keep making promises.

Don't Say No

We constantly flirted for over a year,
Suddenly we seized the moment squashing our fear;

Reluctantly, we gently hugged and passionately
kissed,
Quickly we realized what we had made each other
miss;

Understanding that we were compromising ourselves,
We knew we couldn't share this affair with anyone
else;

How beautiful the moments treasured in heart,
After over a year, we finally past start;

Together we can write a new script or song,
Even though we acknowledge what we are doing is
wrong;

With patience and guidance, it can be made right,
And what we are doing in the dark can be embraced
in the light;

I cannot see why you want to pull back and separate
us,
I would rather you take some time, get yourself
together, if you must;

But I won't allow you to simply walk away from me,
Especially since I have shared myself with you so
freely;

It will be difficult for you to erase me from your
thoughts and life,
Of course, the final decision is yours, one I cannot
override;

Because even though I don't want you to say no,
I would rather separate as a friend than foe.

There are times when a loss whether it is within or outside of our control, it forces us to mourn. Sometimes it is a breakup, other times it is a death.

We all reach stages in our lives when we must make life altering decisions. It is those times when we control our own destiny.

Every experience is a chance to learn something new and apply those lessons to more challenging events that will most likely occur in our lives.

In this chapter, words are used to reach into the depths of the inner spirit to provide inspirational support, emotional stability and motivation for individuals to hold steadfast to their convictions.

Taking Control

Without the intimacy of love, my life's been in a
drought,
Chasing dreams, coming to forks, and choosing the
wrong routes;

So many times I have made the wrong choices, and
now my life's a mess,
Those decisions were mine, I'm guilty, I plead no
contest;

To defend myself, I ask for just one chance to
explain,
How I am taking control of my life and there is going
to be a change;

I have managed to dream again, and look forward to
tomorrow,
A brighter future for me, with no room for sorrow;

I have redirected, adjusted and focused myself well,
From the words I speak, it is easy to tell;

That I know what I want, and I know what I need,
To be happy in this world and to succeed;

I have got to stand up, be counted, and take control
of my future,
And accept the fact that in life, nothing is for sure.

A Spell

Collectively we know things are going downhill,
Yet it has not changed the way that I feel;

My, how people change quickly in this day and time,
The violence, drugs and divorce rate all should be
crimes;

Our precious children are the ones that are last,
The ones who cry when they feel like outcasts;

They search for a place to carve and call their own,
But no matter how they search, they still end up
alone;

What can we do to change this bad wind?
Is there anyone out there who can help them start
again?

So much time has passed and dignity lost,
And for our mistakes, these children pay the cost;

Sometimes we sincerely can't protect the ones we
hold dear,
We watch them suffer day by day, year after year;

If only we held that wonderful magic wand and could
cast a spell,
So instantly these children could live a fairy tale;

That spell could make life easier for them to deal
with,
And heal their family as though it was a hundred year
old quilt.

53

If Only

Resounding resistance to more than a friendship,
Questions about fidelity, love, temptation and the
meaning of a kiss;

To circumvent or to simply pretend it doesn't exist,
To discover the magic of perhaps what was missed;

What do we do with these wondering thoughts?
Give in to the vision and temptation, because they are
not our fault;

Bask in the moment of visiting again in heart and
mind,
Rejoice in the fact that you're learning each other for
the first time;

Don't sell yourself short by continuing to wonder,
Don't second guess yourself or even ponder;

Should you do this or should you do that?
Just take every chance to dwell on the fact;

That you have become friends after such a long
while,
That you feel at ease with yourself and comfortable
with his style;

It's the way things are, the way they should be,
When love and acceptance are more than perceived;

If you spend too much time considering your actions,
The best you can do is develop reactions;

The spontaneity will disappear, the spur of the
moment will pass,
You'll miss a chance to create a memory to last;

A lifetime of wondering how things could have been,
If only you had decided to become more than friends.

Dare to Dream

Setting goals, putting in the time and hard work to achieve those goals,
Is what sets the successful people apart from those who turn up their nose;

People who dare to dream are open minded and willing to learn,
They lead the way with role model leadership, defining the road map for their turn;

At work, at life, at success and at a chance to help others achieve,
People who dare to dream are successful because they believe;

In themselves, their values and in others,
They do not see people in color, only as sisters and brothers;

People who dare to dream could care less where you or I are from,
Because they know that we all march to the beat of the same drum;

There is something to be learned and gained from everyone's life,
It's up to you as an individual to develop love in yourself and take some pride;

To be whatever you dare to be,
Remember it all starts with a simple dream.

Styles

As the water flows from a fountain,
So does snow melt and flow down a mountain;

Fads come in and fads move on,
So do the trends in clothes, speech and homes;

Remember when you move, exude class and style,
Because your impression will linger on for a while;

People will remember you decades from now and
someone will undoubtedly mention,
How you magnetized people and got their attention;

So be careful what you say, but more importantly
watch what you do;
Because you had better believe, somebody's always
watching you.

Lift Your Head

How are you going to find a way out,
When your eyes are always facing south?

There is nothing down there, nothing good,
Lift your head to Jesus if you would;

For He is the light, the leader of the true way,
All you have to do is bend your knees and pray;

Lift your head to heaven, call on His name,
For believing in Christ does not lead to shame;

How convenient He is when you are in trouble,
How dependable He is to come on the double;

To relieve your burden, your grief and despair,
Because He is your Father and He really does care;

For you are His child in this troubled land,
And you will make it through if you just hold His hand.

He'll be there for you, He's never failed,
Lift your head to Jesus, because He always prevails.

"AS HIS CHILD, DON'T BE DISCOURAGED, SAD OR EVEN CRY.
DON'T EVEN BE DOWNHEARTED, AND HERE'S THE REASON WHY:

You have a GOD who is almighty, sovereign and supreme. You have a GOD who loves you and He chose you for his team."

Remember... LIFT YOUR HEAD.

Treat a Black Woman

Treat a black woman with class,
It is the only way to make up for her past;

Treat a black woman like you would want her to treat
you,
Because she has already endured enough abuse;

Treat a black woman like the queen she was born to
be,
Endow her with love, respect and the support that she
needs;

Then maybe she will rise in society where she
belongs,
Because she has already proven that she is more than
black, she's beautiful and strong.

You Make Me Laugh

I don't know how you do it, but you make me laugh,
Even though we share so much, our personalities still
clash;

I yearn to spend more and more time with you,
To allow the love we share an opportunity to
continue;

I don't know how you do it, but you bring joy to my
heart,
I could brainstorm for answers, but I don't know
where to start;

Maybe it is the smile on your face as you look into my
eyes,
Maybe it is the way you kiss my hand, never once, but
twice;

Or maybe it is the way you share your most inner
thoughts with me,
Or the way you say I love you so freely;

I don't know how you do it, but you make me love
you crazily,
So crazy that I want you in my life an eternity;

I don't know how you do it, but I want you to make
me laugh for the rest of my life,
As we build our lives together, you - husband, me -
wife.

Prejudice Cuts Like Glass

I come from a strong, proud heritage in a far away
land,
My ancestors were manipulated, beaten and then
drug in American sand;

This hatred is documented in films, movies, books,
and oral speech from generation to generation,
For too many years, because of race, people were
educated, fed, and even lived in separation;

Time has healed some things and enabled some
people to move forward,
But with hate crimes still being committed, we must
continue to call on the Lord;

I love ALL people and life, so much that I try very
hard to be strong,
But sometimes because of the actions of others, I
would rather be alone;

How do I move on? How do I get past…
The things they've done, the words they've said,
when they continue to cut like glass?

Oh God, help me leave everything that's happened to
my family behind,
Show me how to gain the peace that I want in my
heart and mind;

Please help me to get past the prejudiced things they
have done, the belittling words they have said, so they
no longer cut like glass.

An Emotional Uplifting

As the days go by and pass like years,
Your strong yet gentle voice drowns away my fears;

Happiness may be near, but for so long, it's been
afar;
Yet from out of my dreams, my thoughts, my prayers,
here you are;

Life is so strange with its many twists and turns,
And every day my mind, my soul, my ears for your
voice yearns;

To some, it's not right to be together, but you said it's
wrong to be apart,
You just don't know how much your gentle, kind
words lighten my heart;

You were an emotional uplifting in me, confidence
quickly built,
On the mere foundation of your belief that I was an
intellectual quilt.

Who Will?

Who will revisit the dream and make it a reality?
Who will live the dream for all eternity?

Who will pick up the torch and run for the dream of
Dr. King,
And let it have no boundaries like a never ending
ring?

Who will speak out for justice NOW and open their
arms with love,
And fight for everyone's rights and defeat
misconceptions?

Who will take a stand against terrorism regardless of
why?
Who will join as brothers and sisters, stand up, speak
out, and even cry,

For the strong individuals who stood up, fought for,
or died for YOUR freedom,
All the while envisioning a dream that one day
equality and justice would come;

The freedom fighters before us deserve our respect
because of their legacy and accomplishments,
They were drum majors for freedom and for justice;

They stood even when they had to stand alone,
Proving that one person could make a difference
overseas or at home;

So where will you stand, what will you do,
When push comes to shove and you're asked for your
view?

Will you answer honestly, regardless of circumstance
OR
Will you turn you back and hope someone else takes
a stand?

Who will? Will you?

Choose

Choose to turn left or to turn right,
Just make sure you keep your goal in sight;

Choose to take the elevator up or down,
Choose to make your face smile instead of frown;

Choose to travel the road of success,
Learn not to settle for anything less;

Choose to take the high road instead of the low,
Choose to find the answer when you don't know;

Choose to reach for the star and conquer the moon,
Choose to build a mansion instead of a room;

For if you let someone else choose for you,
You have chosen to be a failure and in each case, you
lose.

In Times of Sorrow

Sometimes when we suffer a loss,
Our first tendency is to assign fault;

We see it as no give and all take,
But God is too wise to make a mistake;

It hurts so much and the pain is so deep,
It seems your only relief is to break down and weep;

There's guidance in His strength and His love,
Just ask and He will send you an angel from above;

A burden lifter to carry you through,
A reminder that He still cares for you;

In your time of trouble, there may be doubt,
Just remember, Jesus is the answer, He will guide you
out;

Out of the darkness into the strength of His arms,
He sends grace and mercy, so you won't be alone.

Searching for the Ever Elusive Happiness

Searching for the ever elusive happiness,
Trying to figure a way out of this mess;

Things are so complicated and hurt so much,
When it is the soul, not the body you want to touch;

You derive at an answer for your personal situation,
But the other person can only deliver a reaction;

You have a voice, a body, a soul,
And you want to play a major part as your story
unfolds;

How minute the corner you have placed yourself in,
Such an unselfish notion, not lovers, just friends;

Searching for the ever elusive happiness, clarity and
direction,
Trying to figure out if your heart needs protection;

You are going in circles on what appears to be a
rollercoaster ride,
And the more you think about it, you are confused
inside;

Yet you search for the ever elusive happiness for a
lifetime,
Be the results good or bad, you take chances, time
after time;

Settle back for a change, let your mind be at ease,
Focus on the obstacles, roll up your sleeves;

Take out all of your problems leaving no trace,
As you take the world by storm and laugh in its face;

Happiness, no matter how elusive it tries to be,
Is just within your reach with patience, time and
faith, because you believe.

Take Your Time

Take your time when you look into my eyes,
Envision two hearts slowly taking flight;

Take your time, when you speak words of joy,
Speak words of encouragement, respect my heart;

Take your time when you are close in more ways than
one,
Relax, take advantage of the situation, have fun;

Take your time when you feel the urge to make
decisions fast,
Reminisce on your experiences, but don't relive the
past;

Because if you rush and don't take your time,
You could possibly lose a chance to capture a heart
and mind;

Someone who could bring prosperity and happiness
to you one day,
A strong hold that would never stray;

Take your time as you ponder what might be
possible,
The thought of loving someone can't be that awful;

Don't sever the ties and let that person go,
Closing the door of possibility means you will never
know;

If the choice you made was good or bad,
If the long term effect will leave you happy or sad;

So take your time, find yourself while you choose to be alone,
Just remember there's a place in someone's heart waiting for you to call home.

Be There, Lord

As we travel this journey with love,
Many blessings are bestowed on us from above;

For together we promised to conquer the world,
To start a family…a boy, a girl;

Stay with us Lord as our way gets dark,
And we face new challenges that we must embark;

Be there, walk with us Lord, don't leave our sides,
Be there, hasten us, don't let us lose our stride;

Be there, keep our eyes focused and our feet firmly
planted,
Be there to keep us true to your word and deeds
without antics;

Never leave us if we should stray,
Be there to help us keep our faith in a brighter day.

Planning for Someone

Are you here? I want you here with me,
Regardless of whether it is meant to be;

I want it to happen and I can deal with it now,
The big question to answer is simply how;

How do we do the right thing and who determines
what is right?
Touching, wanting and planning for someone
tonight;

Dreaming of who it could be and having them slip
through my hands,
Trying desperately to hold on, respect and
understand;

That I am waiting for someone who may never come,
Yet I plan to melt in the comfort of their arms;

I am contemplating scenarios that might present
themselves,
I see happiness as we focus on ourselves;

I plan to fight for what I want and take a chance on
someone who may be good,
I won't question myself, I will be confident as I
should;

Are you planning for someone who will never do
anything to hurt you?
Planning for that person to be honest and always tell
the truth;

Then plan for someone who will never place you on a shelf,
Not unless they were planning to be there themselves;

Planning for it to be a rest stop as you continue your journey for peace and pleasure,
Creating memories and moments that both of you will treasure.

One of God's Greatest Blessings

Because God takes the time to create angels that He gives to us through birth to love and care for,

You are now charged with the challenges of mother, role model, and care taker to this new baby.

Congratulations!!!

Your baby is one of God's Greatest Blessings.

Signs of the Times: Twentieth Year Reunion

Can you believe it? We're gathered after twenty years,
Take a look at each other and yourself, wait a
minute...no tears;

You see Signs of the Times.

Some of us are larger, excuse me...full figured, others
are smaller (weight watchers) than before,
But honestly, we do look better than we did twenty
years ago;

You have heard the saying, "What goes around
comes around,"
And "If you keep something long enough, it will
come back in style,"
Some examples of these signs of the times:
In the late 70s, bell-bottoms and air fros gave us
pizzazz,
Time was always short, these things would soon pass;

Did you think you'd be around to see people wearing
one of them again?
Or that people you disliked, despised or hated, would
grow to be your friend?

Signs of the Times

Many of us set goals for ourselves, reached some, but
still striving for others,
Stop. Take a deep breath, now turn to each other...
Aren't you glad, even proud that you put forth the
effort and money to be here?

After all, there's only one chance to celebrate a
whopping twenty years.

Remember how we told ourselves and our parent,
"I'll never say (or do) that to my child."
But you have and you do, I see that smug smile;

Signs of the times

You've grown into a clone of your father or your
mother,
I'm speaking to you, don't look around at each other.

Example:
"If you don't sit down somewhere, I'll knock you to
kingdom come!"
I'm guilty of saying it, but where is kingdom from?

You get the picture and you know what I mean,
Things and people are not always what they seem;

We have classmates and friends doing the best they
can,
They're not here tonight because of circumstances,
which we try to understand;

Signs of the times

Twenty years ago, we were selfish, self-centered, and
thought of no one else,
Well, after two decades, we've grown and developed a
stronger inner self;
Grew up through the fight for Civil Rights, black
power, prejudice, and affirmative action,
For many of us the fight continues, not with
vengeance, but with passion;

76

We're still in the fight for equal this and equal that
within the law,
Remove the glass ceiling, the cork in the bottle, heck,
just give me the 40 acres and a mule, huh!
Okay, maybe just the 40 acres.

On a personal, less serious, but ethnic note,
Ladies, we twist, braid, even wear weave,
All designed to keep our schedules and minds at
ease;

It's the signs of the times, because men enjoy some of
the same looks too,
Don't look around at others, you know I speak the
truth;

Hip huggers, hot pants, and mini-skirts,
Thongs so thin and tight, you know they have to hurt;

Most of these things have gone out, but have found
their way back in fashion,
Close your eyes, visualize, you can't even imagine,

What you looked like when you graduated twenty
years ago,
Some of us did things back then that we don't want
anyone to know;

We experienced a great deal of happiness, joy and
sorrow then and there,
Tell us all how you have been, be open and share;

And as you get those addresses, phone numbers, and
promise to keep in touch,

Remember, *Signs of the Times*... which is why I am glad to see you again, because I've missed you so very much.

Someone to Love

Send me someone to love, someone to love and hold,
An angel from above, I need someone to love and
love me;

Please stand by my side, Lord please be my guide,
Send me someone to love, I need someone to love
and love me;

When he comes in my life, please help me decide that
he is the one for me,
'Cause I need someone to love, someone to love and
love me;

Lord, please hold my hand, help me understand,
Why I have no man to love me,
'Cause I need someone to love, someone to love and
love me;

Someone to run to my arms, someone to keep me
warm, someone to help me be strong,
'Cause I need someone to love, someone to love and
love me.

HE Continues to Love Me

No matter how late on HIM I call,
When my fight with life turns into a brawl;
HE is always there to break and cradle my fall,
HE continues to love me, HE continues to love me.

No matter how low I seem to be,
HE always manages to come and comfort me;
It's been so long since HE died on Calvary,
                    MY LORD,
HE continues to love me, HE continues to love me.

When you aim for the moon and land among the
stars,
When you fall so low, you don't know where you are;
HE will pick you up and guide you from afar,
'Cause HE continues to love you, HE continues to
love you.

So take a deep breath while you stand still,
Believe in your heart that HIS word and work is real;
Be patient as GOD performs HIS will,
'Cause, HE continues to love you, HE continues to
love me.

No matter what's going on, HE is there for you,
When you're in trouble, HE will pull you through;
Just remember how much HE has blessed you,
'Cause HE continues to love you, HE continues to
love you.
                    And...
            HE continues to love me,
            HE continues to love me.

www.ingramcontent.com/pod-product-compliance
Lightning Source LLC
Chambersburg PA
CBHW032027040426

42448CB00006B/743